CONTENTS

DIY UFO POEM

Acrostic (variation)
Judith Nicholls

Umbrella Fights Officer?
Unapproachable Fish Offside?
Uncanny Frog Objects?

Unfold Furled Omelette?
Unattached Fabulous Oarsman?
Underpants Fumigate Oldham?

THE UNiDENTiFiED FrYiNG OMELETTE

This bo

Collected by Andrew Fusek Peters
Illustrations by Chris Mould

HODDER
Wayland

CLERIHEW

Clerihew, Penny Kent

Andrew Fusek Peters
Measures words in feet and metres.
It's not their length he likes to measure –
Poetic standards are his pleasure.

Acknowledgements

'DIY UFO Poem', 'Football' © Judith Nicholls 2000, reprinted by permission of the author; 'Taking The Plunge' © John Mole, taken from *Boo To A Goose* (Peterloo Poets 1987); 'Dad, The Amateur Hypnotist' © Mike Johnson, first appeared in *Ridiculous Relatives* ed. Paul Cookson (Macmillan, 1999); 'Lim' © Gerard Benson, first published in *Does It Trouble You?* ed. Gerard Benson (Viking, Puffin) reprinted by permission of the author; 'Play No Ball' is part of *Tower Block Poet* by Gerard Benson, commissioned by BBC Radio for the series Critical Language, reprinted by permission of the author; 'River' from *Cows Moo, Calves Toot* (© Viking, 1995) by June Crebbin; 'The Acrostic Valentine' © John Whitworth, first published in *The Complete Poetical Works of Phoebe Flood* (Hodder 1997) reprinted by permission of the author.

Wth thanks to all other authors, whose poems are reprinted with their permission.

© Copyright Hodder Children's Books 2000

Editorial Project Management:
Mason Editorial Services
Designer: Tim Mayer

Published in 2000 by
Hodder Wayland, an imprint of
Hodder Children's Books

A Catalogue record for this book is available from the British Library.

ISBN 0 7502 3164 5

Printed and bound in Portugal

Hodder Children's Books
A division of Hodder Headline Ltd.
338 Euston Road, London NW1 3BH

Now try your own DIY UFO Poem!

upside down, unlikely
united, uncle, uncanny
uncertain, ultimate, unbolt
unbeaten, unbutton
unaware, unassuming
unapproachable, unable
umbrella, under, ugly
unattached, ultimate
unwind, unscramble
unmentionable, uncork
unconscious, unlikely
underground, unique
underpants, unfold
undeveloped
understand, underground
unfreeze, unbeaten
unzip, uproarious
upgrade, unskilled
underwater, undress
underarm, umpire
ukelele, ulcers
unicycle, unmask, use
usher, utensil, unload
upset, U-turn
ungovernable

fade, fish
fashionable, fabric
fabulous, face, facts
fiddle, fail, fair, fare
fat, fall, false, fame
feel, faint, ferocious
fit, fill, film, fine, find
fix, first, fighting
free, fritter, frog, fry
fuse, funnel, fuzzy
futuristic, fun, flood
flatten, fly, fume
follow, foggy, front
fumigate, form, foul
frolic, friendly,
frequently, frizzle
flibberty-gibbet
first, formidable
forlorn, foreign
French, foolish
foreboding, force
forget, forge, forfeit
fraudulent
film, Filofax
flummoxed

obligation, oak,
oath, oarsman
oar, oatmeal
obedient, obelisk
obesity, oboe
observation, oil
obnoxious, ode
obscure, okapi
observant, ocean
obsession, offer
obsolete, obstacle
obstinacy, office
obvious, occasion
occupation, other
occupant, October
octuplets, oddball
odd, offence
official, offside
offshore, offspring
okay, Oldham
Olympic, omelette
one-stop, ozone
ooze, opposite
onomatopoeia
outrageous

UNIDENTIFIED   FLYING   OBJECT

SWARM PRAISE

Acrostic, Philip Waddell

Busy
Engineers of
Exquisite
Sweetness.

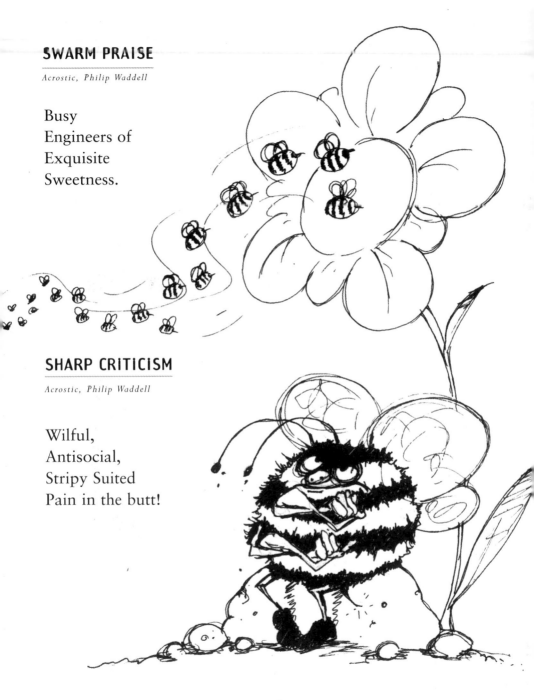

SHARP CRITICISM

Acrostic, Philip Waddell

Wilful,
Antisocial,
Stripy Suited
Pain in the butt!

THE ACROSTIC VALENTINE

Acrostic, John Whitworth

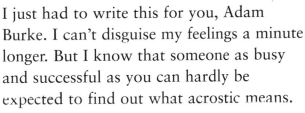

I just had to write this for you, Adam
Burke. I can't disguise my feelings a minute
longer. But I know that someone as busy
and successful as you can hardly be
expected to find out what acrostic means.

Wonderfully
Handsome,
Attractively
Tanned,

Amazingly

Brilliant,
Incredibly
Grand,

Dearly
Adorable,
Fearlessly
True,

Witty
And
Loveable
Lusciously
YOU!

7

ME ONE, VILLA NIL

Villanelle, Dave Calder

As I sit quiet in my seat
with pencil in hand, out of sight
I'm scoring a goal with my feet.

Our team is close to defeat
when I take this pass from the right
as I sit quiet in my seat.

I might look unbothered and neat
but inside I'm wild with delight –
I'm scoring a goal with my feet.

Though I'm staring at a blank sheet
I run upfield with all my might
as I sit quiet in my seat.

A great shot! Fast and low, it beat
the goalie! So hard to sit tight
when scoring a goal with my feet.

I wish I was out on the street
not in here, pretending to write.
As I sit quiet in my seat
I'm scoring a goal with my feet.

SHELL VILLANELLE

Villanelle, Tony Mitton

I am a snail. This shell is where I hide.
The world is full of danger, threat and spite.
My brittle canopy feels safe inside.

My way is slow. A snail's pace I slide.
I have no speed, no means of sudden flight.
I am a snail. This shell is where I hide.

With steady caution through the world I glide.
If shadows loom, or things flash fast and bright,
my brittle canopy feels safe inside.

I cannot parry stabbing beaks with pride,
nor wear my armour like a valiant knight.
I am a snail. This shell is where I hide.

If jabbing birds should come, all glitter-eyed,
I have no way to stand at bay and fight.
My brittle canopy feels safe inside.

But for this case, I'd long ago have died.
And so this spell I steadily recite:
I am a snail. This shell is where I hide.
My brittle canopy feels safe inside.

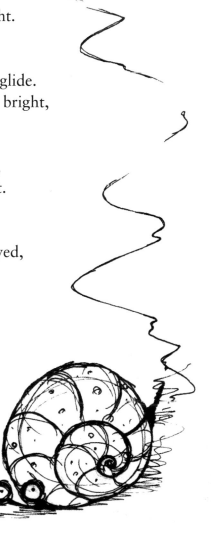

IN TRAINING

Boustrophedon or Ox-writing, Andrew Fusek Peters

The Sure-footed train weaves side to side
stride Striker's this by slips land
Telegraph poles are the referee's guide,
wide so net the like yawn mouths and

The crowd is going clackety clack,
attack under is mile by mile
Snoozing faces going slack
track the down offside an there's while

A hundred whistles screech delay
play halted have line on leaves
The train is sulking, calls it a day,
way his get can't he that grieves

Cinquain, Judith Nicholls (Sorry, NOT a football fan!)

Simple!
Kick round object
over long muddy field.
Try to aim it between two sticks –
for kicks!

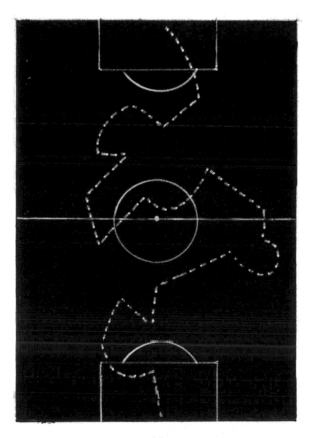

HIGH COO HAIKU

Haiku, Tony Mitton

White dove in the blue,
perched up there against the sky,
sings high, high, high coo.

UNTITLED

Haiku, Moritake (Sixteenth-century poet)

The falling flower
I saw drift back to the branch
Was a butterfly.

YELLOW CROCUSES

Haiku, Jill Townsend

Yellow crocuses
push their crayons through the frost,
drawing attention.

HAIKU

Haiku, Peggy Poole

Half-time score: Nil Nil
Ravenous, the goal mouth gapes
Longing for a ball.

UNTITLED

Haiku, Ian Souter

Electricity's
current problem is its
shocking behaviour!

HIKER 2

Haiku, Ian McMillan

Walked seventeen miles
then had a long rest on this
old Japanese form.

13

SHAKESPEARE'S 18TH WORM

Sonnet (Parody), Celia Warren

Shall I compare thee to a bit of string?
Thou art more bristly and more flexible.
Rough soils do hold the horrid stones that sting
And cruel clay is heavily inedible.

Sometime too wet the mouth of heaven spits,
And often are the segments clogged with dirt,
And every squirm from squirm sometime desists,
By chance of nature's sending in a bird.

But thy eternal wriggle shan't grow weak,
Nor lose possession of that squirm thou hast,
Nor blackbird brag thou danglest from his beak,
When in eternal stringiness thou growest.

So long as worms can squirm or hedgehogs fast,
So long as birds are late your life will last.

SHALL I COMPARE THEE TO A SUMMER'S DAY?

Sonnet, William Shakespeare

Shall I compare thee to a summer's day?
Thou art more lovely and more temperate:
Rough winds do shake the darling buds of May,
And summer's lease hath all too short a date:
Sometime too hot the eye of Heaven shines,
And often is his gold complexion dimm'd:
And every fair from fair sometime declines,
By chance, or nature's changing course, untrimm'd.
But thy eternal summer shall not fade
Nor lose possession of that fair thou owest;
Nor shall Death brag thou wanderest in his shade,
When in eternal lines to time thou growest;
So long as men can breathe, or eyes can see,
So long lives this, and this gives life to thee.

THE AMOROUS TEACHER'S SONNET TO HIS LOVE

Sonnet, Dave Calder

Each morning I teach in a daze until
the bell that lets me hurry down and queue
with pounding heart to wait for you to fill
my eyes with beauty and my plate with stew.
Dear dinner lady, apple of my eye,
I long to shout I love you through the noise
and take your hand across the shepherd's pie
despite the squealing girls or snickering boys.
O let us flee together and start up
a little cafe somewhere in the Lakes
and serve day trippers tea in china cups
and buttered scones on pretty patterned plates.

Alas for dreams so rudely bust in two –
some clumsy child's spilt custard on my shoe.

MISS EAGLE

Clare Bevan (with thanks to Lord Tennyson)
Tercets of triple rhyme (Parody)

She picks her prey with practised skill,
Pounces on pupils small and still,
Freezes their blood with comments shrill.

The frightened class before her sighs,
She fools them with her strict disguise –
And no one notes her nervous eyes.

THE EAGLE

Tercets of triple rhyme, Alfred, Lord Tennyson

He clasps the crag with crooked hands;
Close to the sun in lonely lands,
Ring'd with the azure world, he stands.

The wrinkled sea beneath him crawls;
He watches from his mountain walls,
And like a thunderbolt he falls.

FRIDAY DUTY

(In which Sir's assembly notices seem spookily similar to 'Pied Beauty')
Clare Bevan

First a plea to Mums for home-made things,
Proud-purple kingly costumes plus a panto cow.

Now glitter-gold certificates for those who swim
In gala-glory, minus water-wings.

Loudly praise ladies who lumpy-lunchtime wow
With spotted puddings, sauce-splashed to the brim,
And nameless spoonfuls, gravy-grey and strange.

Our football team, brave-beaten, take a bow
With sporting smiles. And last, our heartfelt hymn
To 'Those in Peril.' Then swift sweat-shirts change
For Gym.

PIED BEAUTY

Gerard Manley Hopkins

Glory be to God for dappled things –
  For skies of couple-colour as a brindled cow;
    For rose-moles all in stipple upon trout that swim;
Fresh-firecoal chestnut-falls; finches' wings;
  Landscape plotted and pieced – fold, fallow, and plough;
    And all trades, their gear and tackle and trim.
All things counter, original, spare, strange;
  Whatever is fickle, freckled (who knows how?)
    With swift, slow; sweet, sour; adazzle, dim;
He fathers-forth whose beauty is past change:
              Praise him.

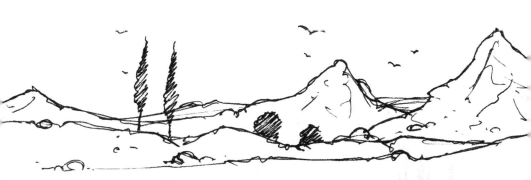

THE PASSIONATE PUPIL DECLARING LOVE

Parody, Andrew Fusek Peters (with thanks to Kit Marlowe)

Come meet with me and after school
Perhaps you'll see that I'm no fool.
If only you would understand,
How I want to hold your hand.

We could walk around the park
Until the day grows old and dark
And on the swings we'll learn to fly
Together we will touch the sky,

And I will make a daisy chain,
Create a crown from drops of rain,
Weave a gown of greenest grass
And watch the hours quickly pass.

As we run home through all the streets,
I shall give you all my sweets.
The singing of the traffic jam
Will tell you how in love I am.

In class your laughter makes me cry
And I just want to ask you why
You think that I am such a fool
To dream of meeting after school.

20

THE PASSIONATE SHEPHERD TO HIS LOVE

Christopher (Kit) Marlowe

Come live with me and be my love,
And we will all the pleasures prove,
That hills and valleys, dales and fields,
And all the craggy mountain yields.

There we will sit upon the rocks,
And see the shepherds feed their flocks,
By shallow rivers to whose falls
Melodious birds sing madrigals.

And I will make thee beds of roses
With a thousand fragrant posies,
A cap of flowers, and a kirtle
Embroidered all with leaves of myrtle;

A gown made of the finest wool
Which from our pretty lambs we pull;
Fair lined slippers for the cold,
With buckles of the purest gold;

A belt of straw and ivy buds,
With coral clasps and amber studs:
And if these pleasures may thee move,
Come live with me and be my love.

The shepherds' swains shall dance and sing
For thy delight each May morning:
If these delights thy mind may move,
Then live with me and be my love.

21

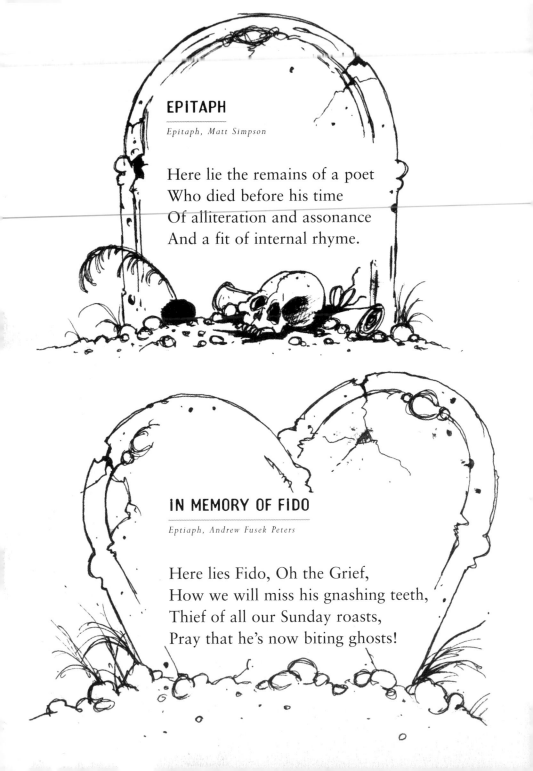

EPITAPH

Epitaph, Matt Simpson

Here lie the remains of a poet
Who died before his time
Of alliteration and assonance
And a fit of internal rhyme.

IN MEMORY OF FIDO

Eptiaph, Andrew Fusek Peters

Here lies Fido, Oh the Grief,
How we will miss his gnashing teeth,
Thief of all our Sunday roasts,
Pray that he's now biting ghosts!

THE SILENT BAND

Virelai Ancien, Jill Townsend

I don't understand
why the local band
   don't play.
The mayor had a hand
in it – he's so grand
   they say –

and there was his bare
head – all red. I swear
   he planned
to take revenge there
and then, and see their
   band banned.

so they never may,
not after that day
   the mayor
got in the band's way,
tubas blew away
   his hair

BOOKWORM BARRY AND THE SOULFUL SESTINAS

Sestina, Andrew Fusek Peters

I couldn't help coming top of the set,
And working hard was never dead
Cool. Jack, the bully, brainless and bad,
Called me one of the *girls*.
I sat silent as a closed-up book,
Thinking of a day I could hit

Back. Bully-boy Jack was a one-hit
Wonder, followed around by his jet-set
Gang that wouldn't know a book
If it walked right up and hit
Them in the gob. How could the girls
Adore him? And never see how bad

He really was? I wanted to get him bad,
And on a hide-my-crying day, I hit
on an idea. Behind their back, Jilting Jack thought girls
Were 'soppy, sissy, obsessed with set-
ting their hair, forever talking about dead-
dull feelings, noses glued to a book!'

Call me a swot, but I got some info in a book;
A tape machine was bought by Barry who bad-
Ly wanted revenge. Jack, the Giant Killer, was dead
In my sights. I told him he was a hit,
Praised his boasting blab. It was a set-
Up. He started mouthing off 'those boring girls...'

I took the tape to his adoring girls,
Who heard and roared 'It's time to book
The bully!' and grabbed him after school. Jet-set
Melted away. 'We're stroppy, not soppy, bold and bad!'
Jack fell on his knees, sobbed 'Please don't hit
Me!' they sneered and said 'You're dead!'

I watched the action, admit to being dead
chuffed, and cheered them on 'Atta-girls!'
Jack, the Giant Wailer wept as they hit
Him on the head with their handbags. Book-
Worm Barry the hero! Jack-the-Bad
Now sobbing and sad. My future was set!

It's not half bad having mates who are girls!
Don't live by the book, or you'll end up dead-
Set in your ways, and sad as last year's hit!

A RONDEL

Rondel, John Kitching

A rondel is painful to write.
It's quite easy to make a mistake,
Like slipping through ice on a lake,
Or falling from bed in the night.

But work hard and it will come right,
You may bake then a rich rondel cake.
A rondel is painful to write.
It's quite easy to make a mistake.

A ballad's bark is much worse than its bite.
A limerick's a rather strange snake
Never tackled by old William Blake.

Fourteen lines, just two rhymes? That is tight!
A rondel is painful to write.
It's quite easy to make a mistake.

THE POET

Englyn, Janis Priestley

What is a poet but a person who
writes words on a page, then
crosses them out with his pen
and puts them back in again.

THE EISTEDDFOD

Englyn, Anon

SONG-HOUSE of all sounding things – high senate
Whence harmony springs,
Which note upon note nature flings
In the flight of the soul from the strings.

27

PANTOUM AND PEAS PLEASE

Pantoum, Andrew Fusek Peters

I could fall in love with food,
A plate of greasy salty chips
Puts me in a brilliant mood,
For edible relationships.

A plate of greasy salty chips
With a can of mushy peas,
For edible relationships
Make me mushy at the knees.

With a can of mushy peas,
I'd even do a hip chip-tease!
Makes me mushy at the knees,
Swimming in the ketchup seas.

I'd even do the hip chip tease,
Or ask a burger for her hand,
Swim in ketchup curdled seas,
Hope that veg would understand.

Ask a burger for her hand,
Wedded in the school canteen,
Hope that veg would understand,
That greens are really not my scene.

Wedded in the school canteen,
A pinch of salt made great confetti,
Though greens are really not my scene,
I'd rather snog spaghetti!

That wedding in the school canteen
Put me in a brilliant mood,
Though greens are really not my scene
I'm in love with fabulous food!

TANKA

Tanka, Katherine Gallagher

Last night, the full moon
hung like a papery lamp
over my quiet road.
I savoured the chilly sky –
the moon tagging my shadow.

29

DOUBLE DACTYL TONGUE TWISTER

Double dactyl, Polly Peters

Utterly-Nutterly
Heart's feeling fluttery,
Matt and Samantha
Met up by the bog.

Matt wasn't brave,
But Samantha just gave him
An extralongsmoochathon
Slurp of a snog!

RIVER

Kenning/Shape poem, June Crebbin

boat–carrier

bark–lapper

home–provider

tree–reflector

leaf–catcher

field–wanderer

stone–smoother

fast–mover

gentle–stroller

sun–sparkler

sea–seeker

THE BOG STANDARD BALLAD

Ballad, Andrew Fusek Peters

As I walked down the corridor
Of crumbling old St Nicks,
One winter night, I heard a sound,
The wind was playing tricks.

My mum was late as usual,
The school was dark as a crow,
My hair stood up on the back of my neck,
Just as I had to 'go'.

There was some gossip of a ghoul
who haunted the boy's bathroom
And howled beyond the creaking door
of his bog-standard tomb.

His name was Jack, and for the crack
In eighteen sixty-two,
On a whim, he went for a swim
In the cistern of the loo.

A boy came along, whistling a song,
Spending a penny and flushed,
Jack not nimble, Jack not quick,
he cried out as he was crushed!

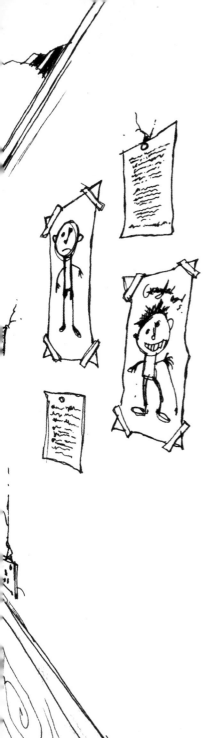

And now a flush came over my face,
I had to get out in the end,
I felt like such a drip, drip, drip,
He was driving me round the u-bend.

I screamed a scream, no sound came out,
The Ghost of Jack was coming,
Closer he came, with a tap, tap, tap
the poltergeist of plumbing!

I turned to jelly, he was a smelly
Creeping kind of soul,
I cried out Mummy! He was a *mummy*,
Wrapped round with toilet roll!

My mum called out, I gave a shout,
I got away scot-free,
Slimy Jack, said 'I'll be back',
And limped off to the lavatory.

Beware the loo-py ghost of St Nicks
Who wails the bathroom blues.
You have to go? It's a total no-no!
Remember what lurks in the loos. . .

LIMERICK

Limerick, J Patrick Lewis

A woman named Mrs S. Claus
Deserves to be heard from because
She sits in her den
Baking gingerbread men
While her husband gets all the applause.

LIM

Limerick, Gerard Benson

There once was a bard of Hong Kong
Who thought limericks were too long.

LIMERICK

Limerick, Anon

An epicure, dining at Crewe,
Found a rather large mouse in his stew;
Said the waiter: 'Don't shout,
Or wave it about,
Or the rest will be wanting one too.'

MAHLER AND THE MARTIANS

Limerick, Nick Toczek

A song-cycle writer called Mahler
Had Martians turn up in his parlour.
They told him, dear reader:
'Take us to your lieder!'
And sung them, though somewhat bizarrely.

LIMERICK

Limerick, Coral E. Copping

Dad waited while Mum bought the ham.
But when she came out, she said: 'Sam!
That one's not our baby!'
He answered: 'Well, maybe,
But look! it's a much nicer pram.'

FISHY STORIES

Limerick, Dave Calder

There was a bright teacher from Torquay
who went to fight sharks in the North Sea.
When asked why he had,
he said "'Cos I'm mad
and it's safer than teaching 4c."

35

TAKING THE PLUNGE

Couplets, John Mole

One day a boy said to a girl in a swimming pool
'I'm going to dive in, are you?' She replied
'No thanks. I bet you can't anyway.' So the boy
got on the diving board and dived and said
'See.' The girl replied 'Flipping eck!'

(Simon Wilkinson)

Flipping eck, cor blimey, strewth,
You're my hero, that's the honest truth.

Lummy, crickey, lordy lord,
It's a long way down from that diving board.

Itchy beard and stone the crows,
Don't you get chlorine up your nose?

Luv a duck and strike me pink,
You're slicker than the soap in the kitchen sink.

Knock me down with a sparrow's feather,
How about us going out together?

Groovy, t'riffic, brill and smashing,
Me 'n' you, we could start things splashing.

Watcha cocky, tara, see ya,
Meet me for a coke in the cafeteria.

Halleluja and Amen,
If you like this poem you can read it again.

LATE FOR A DATE

Couplets, Andrew Fusek Peters

Toasty dreams have crumbled away,
To the cornflake dawn of day;

Birds sing loud as a kettle on the boil,
I wriggle from bed like a worm out of soil.

As sunlight pours a cup of tea
The mist is rising, just like me;

Shiver like a fridge, wait in the queue,
Traffic jam outside the loo.

Clothes laid out like butter on bread,
Squeeze them on like sandwich spread!

Hungry as a horse, maybe too late
Gallop downstairs, await my fate.

Mum looks sour, but Dad's so sweet,
He saved my bacon! Time to eat!

WHITE KNUCKLE RIDE

Terza rima, Jill Townsend

I close my eyes, imagine I'm an astronaut.
Everyone else is screaming but you won't catch me
looking afraid, no chance. Is this the way they're taught

to deal with weightlessness I wonder. I can see
Mum with the pram and Uncle Martin way down there,
but upside down. It seems like an eternity

since we were all the right way round. It was a dare,
my brother said: I couldn't let him down. So here
I am, hung like a bat, suspended in the air

sixty feet up. But one thing is becoming clear –
about that piece of pizza, with tomatoes, cheese,
the anchovies and so on – it could reappear.

And so I think I'd like to get off quickly please.

THE USE OF BOOKS

Terza rima sonnet, Jenny Morris

Books open random windows, sudden doors
on scenes of sorcery, on seven seas,
on alien outer space, on ancient wars,

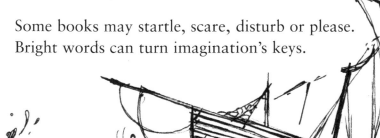

so we can view the far antipodes,
or understand the thoughts of brilliant men,
or fly with strangers on a high trapeze.

It only takes one gifted writer's pen
to move us to another place or time
to meet a different world as it was then.

So in Olympus learn what is sublime,
perhaps in Hades cross the Styx with ease,
or creep with beings from primeval slime.

Some books may startle, scare, disturb or please.
Bright words can turn imagination's keys.

PLAY NO BALL

Thin poem, Gerard Benson

What a wall!
Play No ball,
It tells us all.
Play No Ball,
By Order!

Lick no lolly.
Skip no rope.
Nurse no dolly.
Wish no hope.
Hop no scotch.
Ring no bell.
Telly no watch.
Joke no tell.
Fight no friend.
Up no make.
Penny no lend.
Hand no shake.
Tyre no pump.
Down no fall.
Up no jump
Name no call.
And...
Play No Ball.
No Ball. No Ball.
BY ORDER!

DAD, THE AMATEUR HYPNOTIST

Mike Johnson

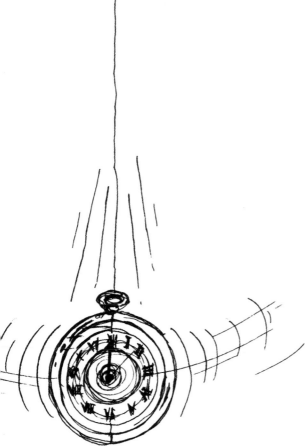

Follow my
swinging watch
with your
eyes. Now
you are
feeling sleepy...
When I
count to
three and
click my
fingers, you
will wake
up, then
bark like
a dog.
One. Two.
Three. Click!

'Miaow.'

THE ORIGIN OF THE CLERIHEW

Clerihew, Roger Stevens

Edmund Clerihew Bentley's fame grew
When he invented the clerihew
But if he wanted a fortune he would have been wise
To invent the double cheeseburger, with fries.

SUPERMAN

Clerihew, Jill Townsend

Superman
helps people wherever he can
and deals with miscreants
by frightening them in his underpants.

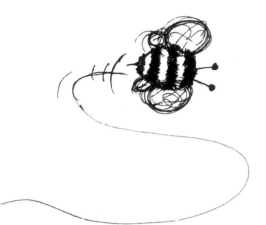

TO BE A BEE?

Triolet, Colin West

To be a bee or not to be
A bee, that is the question.
You see, I'm in a quandary.
"To be a bee or not to be
A bee" is what perplexes me,
Pray, What is your suggestion?
To be a bee or not to be
A bee, that is the question.

BIRD-WATCHING

Triolet, Catherine Benson

How to tell a rook from crow?
Quite simple really, if you look
And find a patch of white you'll know
How to tell a rook from crow.
It's bald skin that you see below
The bill. If not, then it's a crow, not rook.
How to tell a rook from crow?
Quite simple really, if you look.

MONSOON MOMENTS

Ghazal, Nasir Kazmi (translated by Debjani Chatterjee)

Once more the monsoon winds blow and I remember you;
Once more the leafy anklets chime and I remember you.

All day I was lost in the maze of worldly affairs;
Now when the sun climbs down the walls, I remember you.

Once more the crow calls in the empty courtyard at home,
Once more the drops of nectar fall – and I remember you.

Once more the herons cry in an ocean of green grass,
The season of yellow blooms has come – and I remember you.

At first I wept aloud, and then began to laugh.
Thunder rolls and lightning flashes – and I remember you.

SUNRISE WILSON

Wilson, Ian McMillan

Such a dazzling sunrise,
A delight for the eyes,
Like a big glowing turnip
A sunrise seems wise:
The dawn's daily prize!

A PALINDROME FOR AND AGAINST HUNTING

Nick Toczek

Evil Won,
We footstep on bats,
Trap a wolf,
Stun deer,
Gas rats.
O! Slay anon!

No! Nay also!
Stars agreed: "Nuts!"
Flow apart. Stab no pets,
Too few now live.

SNOW WILSON

Wilson, Ian McMillan

Snow like a white hat
On the high-rise flat
White as mashed potato
Or a white welcome mat
Or Mrs Smith's cat.

Understanding different kinds of poem

Rhyme scheme: in a poem, each new rhyme at the end of the line is labelledwith a letter from the alphabet, e.g. The Passionate Pupil Declaring Love is AABB CCDD etc.

Stanza: a single verse of a poem. Poems are generally made up of a number of stanzas.

Acrostic – A poem where the first letters of each line make up a separate word or sentence relating to the subject of the poem.

Ballad (from the Latin *Ballare*, 'to Dance') – Song, lyric or rhythmic poem that often tells a sad or ghostly story. Can be in four-line stanzas, rhyming ABCBDEFE etc. The ballad is for reading, performing aloud and singing, and usually follows a de-dum, de-dum rhythm, known as iambic metre.

Boustrophedon or Ox-writing – A poem where the first line reads left to right and the second line right to left, etc.

Cinquain – Invented by Adelaide Crapsey, this is a poem with five lines of 2, 4, 6, 8 and 2 syllables.

Clerihew – A quatrain about a famous person in two couplets rhyming AABB, with the first line ending in the famous person's name. The trick is to rhyme their name.

Couplets – A traditional form used by Shakespeare, Milton etc. Stanzas of two lines rhyming AA BB CC etc., often written with 10 syllables per line (which is called Iambic Pentameter).

Double Dactyl – Two quatrains, the first three lines of which are two dactyls, the fourth a dactyl followed by a stressed syllable. A dactyl is a stressed syllable followed by two unstressed syllables. So, the dactyllic rhythm sounds like dum-diddy, dum-diddy etc. Line 1 rhymes with line 4.

is a nonsense word. The line before the end is often just 1 word.

Englyn – A traditional Welsh form of 30 syllables in 4 lines with 10 syllables on line 1 followed by 6, 7 and 7 on lines 2, 3 and 4. The rhyme is ABBB, but often with an internal rhyme (i.e. a rhyme that doesn't occur at the line end) in line 1 to rhyme with the following 3 line endings.

Epitaph – A short poem in memory of someone or an animal who has died. Often put on tombstones. Not always serious!

Kenning – An Anglo-Saxon way of looking at the world through metaphor. For instance, the sea was known as a whale road, or today as a beach snogger!

Haiku – In Japan, haiku came from *hokku*, the first verse of a much longer poem called a *renga*. A haiku has 17 syllables divided into 3 lines of 5, 7, and 5 syllables. Traditional forms often contain a *kigo* (word referring to a season).

Ghazal – An ancient Persian form of couplets which don't have to rhyme. The last phrase or words in line 1 are repeated at the end of each couplet. The last couplet sometimes mentions the writer's name. The ghazal is a lyrical poem, often romantic and mystical, whose couplets each exhibit an independence and completeness. The ghazal is recited, and sometimes sung, at a *mushaira* or gathering of poets where the audience gives an immediate response to each couplet.

Limerick – A humorous verse with 3 long lines and 2 short, which rhymes AABBA.

Palindrome – A poem that reads the same backwards as it does forwards. A feat of imagination!

Pantoum – A set of quatrains with line 2 and line 4 in stanza 1 repeated as lines 1 and 3 in stanza 2 and so on. The final stanza puts line 1 and 3 of stanza 1 as lines 2 and 4.

Parody – A modern-day version of a classical poem that copies the structure for humorous or lyrical effect.

Rondel – Fourteen lines with only two rhymes throughout, rhyming ABBA, ABAB ABBAAB. The first

2 lines are repeated at the end of the second quatrain, and in the last 2 lines of the poem.

Sestina – Six stanzas of 6 lines each ending with a tercet (a three-line stanza). Sestinas don't normally rhyme, but the end words of the first stanza are repeated as the end words of the following stanzas in strict order. See Barry and the Soulful Sestinas (page 2) and work out the order in which end words are repeated! Note how the last tercet must contain all 6 of these words.

Sonnet – An Italian thirteenth-century form. The English or Shakespearean Sonnet is 14 lines of 3 quatrains and a couplet, rhyming ABAB CDCD EFEF GG. The final couplet often sums up the poem or adds a twist.

Tanka – This Japanese form is 5 lines long. Lines 1 and 3 have 5 syllables, the others have 7 syllables.

Terza Rima – Stanzas of 3 lines each with the rhyme scheme ABA BCB CDC etc. linking them together.

Thin Poem – Very short lines going down the page make a poem look thin and hungry!

Triolet – A type of rondel: 2 quatrains with 2 rhymes ABAAABAB. Line 1 is repeated as lines 4 and 7, line 2 is repeated as the last line.

Villanelle – Three-line stanzas and a quatrain (a four-lined stanza) to finish. The rhyme scheme is ABA ABA ABA ABA ABAA. The first and third lines of the first stanza are repeated at the end of each stanza in different order until the last quatrain, where these 2 lines are put together to make the final couplet.

Virelai Ancien – A French form: stanzas with long lines rhyming with each other and short lines rhyming with each other. The short lines make the rhyme of the long lines in the next stanza, and the last stanza has the short lines rhyming with the long lines of the first stanza – e.g. AABAAB BBCBBC CCACCA.

Wilson – 'Invented by Herbert Wilson (1817–1888). Five lines which rhyme, apart from the third line which must contain a non-rhyming reference to a vegetable. Actually I made all that up!' – *Ian Macmillan.*